SET GOALS, C(
AND BE

My
GRIT
JOURNAL

KERRY BROWN

KERRY BROWN
WRITER

MY GRIT JOURNAL

MY SAFE PLACE
TO REFLECT, EXPLORE
AND GROW...

This journal belongs to:

Emily

My journey began on:

06.01.21

ENDORSEMENTS

Since I started working to develop grit, I am so much more confident when it comes to starting something new. I know now that success takes time, not talent.

Elise, age 14

I have been using a journal to help me think about and write down how I'm doing for a while because I wanted to become more confident. I now know that I have become more confident because I talk more freely in English and Drama. I have learnt that with the right mindset I can change things.

Emily-Jade, age 12

Success is not about what you know it's about goal-setting and hard work.

Lewis, age 13

I have been working to develop my grit because I wanted to change and improve focus at school and plan homework better. I know that I have improved in English and I am now planning my homework better. I now know that I can change if I put my mind to it and try hard.

Molly, age 12

Learning about grit and the importance of mindset really helped me to regain focus and enthused me to work my butt off and meet my deadlines. I have received my grades for the work I was behind on and I am over the moon, hard work pays off.

Kate, student

Learning about grit has helped me keep trying. At first, I didn't understand algebra but now I have the confidence to try and make mistakes. Now I think I can learn anything about algebra.

Kiyomi, age 13

Before I learnt about the importance of grit I thought I was rubbish at maths. Now I understand how I learn and about neuroplasticity, so I know that I can get smarter in maths. I now challenge myself every day.

Corbin, age 11

Now I have a better understanding of grit and mindset, I accept that to be successful I have to work hard and practice.

Josh, age 14

I thought that other students were naturally better at certain things than me like sport. Now I realise that they just practice {sic} more. To be successful I now know it's more about hard work and effort than talent.

Ben, age 14

By developing more grit, I now accept that it's okay to be different and that anything is possible.

Luke age 18

For #TeamBrown
My heart, my soul and my life.

With thanks to students at Noadswood School

CONTENTS

ABOUT THE AUTHOR, KERRY BROWN

I believe in Grit. Grit is what sets successful people apart from those who just 'make do'. My passion for helping young people develop grit is a result of working as a teacher for over twenty years. The young people I have worked with have all been unique individuals, yet every single one has found an aspect of their life difficult at one point or another. What they needed to face challenges or to help them to be more successful was grit, and that is what I helped them develop. It is such an important life skill, and I'm excited to show you how to get more grit throughout this journal.

I have over twenty years' experience in education – from classroom teacher to headteacher. I have worked with a variety of ages and abilities and now want to use this knowledge and experience to reach out to more young people, people just like you, to help them become the best that they can be.

Having left teaching in 2016, I now run a successful Education, Coaching and Consultancy business, Go Fish Education, in Bournemouth with my husband Dylan. We have the best job in the world as we spend time working with children and adults, coaching them to reach their potential. This might be in terms of improving performance at school/work or it might be to help them find solutions to things they are finding difficult. We also train teachers in growth mindset theory and how to ensure their students reach their potential in the classroom. To date, hundreds of adults and children have benefitted from our advice, support and expertise.

Alongside my love of learning, I write a successful blog, Mrs Brown's Blogs, which was a finalist in the UK Blog Awards in 2017 and 2018, and I have also been nominated for a Successful Woman in Business Award in 2018.

Beyond my professional life, I love nothing more than being with my family, enjoying the company of friends, and when our British weather permits, camping in the Purbecks enjoying the simplicity of life and its surroundings.

BEFORE YOU BEGIN YOUR GRIT JOURNEY

"BECOMING IS BETTER THAN BEING"

Carol Dweck
Professor of Psychology

WHAT CAN THIS JOURNAL DO FOR YOU?

This journal has been designed to help you grow. It is yours to use as you wish and share as you want. In today's busy world, we sometimes forget to take time out for ourselves, time to think about what we really want in life and how we can get it. This journal is your time and space to document your achievements and challenges each week. Use it weekly, to help you make sense of and reflect on where you are right now, where you want to be, what you have achieved and goal-set for the future. Your Grit Journal can help you take charge of your life and make sure you are going in the direction you really want to.

This journal is about you, for you. A place for you to be honest, reflective and aspirational.

Remember, you are doing this because YOU want to. Not because your parents, your teachers or your friends told you to. This is about YOU for YOU. By using My Grit Journal, you will become the best person YOU can be.

I am so excited about this journey you are about to embark on. Your Grit Journal will help you become the best you can, on your terms, at your pace. Sit back buckle up and enjoy the ride!

WHAT IS GRIT?

Grit is something we all have but is often undeveloped. Grit is simply the motivation, that inner drive and determination to keep trying even when things are really tough. You have probably been in a situation where you had to do something that was really challenging, and you had two choices: 1 to give up or 2 to grit your teeth, dig deep and get on with it. People without grit have to give up, they have no other option.

Grit is the ability to face difficult situations with sheer determination to succeed, no matter what. As Angela Duckworth, American academic and psychologist says, "Enthusiasm is common. Endurance is rare."

WHY DO YOU NEED GRIT?

The world can be a tough and confusing place for young people. Daily demands from teachers, family and friends can sometimes feel overwhelming and all-consuming. You need space and solitude to work through these demands and challenges. Grit is what you need to accept and tackle these daily challenges head-on.

The most successful people are where they are today because of their huge levels of grit. Take Will Smith or JK Rowling. Both of these highly successful superstars did not get where they are by accident. They got there because they possessed grit. When times were tough, they did not give up; when they got rejected or experienced failure, they picked themselves up and tried even harder. They didn't let anyone tell them they couldn't do something, they just kept trying in the belief that one day they would definitely get there. Now they inspire others to work hard and set goals in order to achieve them.

WHY KEEP A GRIT JOURNAL?

So here you are at the start of an amazing journey that will help and empower you to become the best person you can be. But 'why should I bother writing a journal? How will that help me develop a grit mindset?' I hear you cry. And yes, you are right to question the relevance and need for this process. You probably have a number of other things you would rather be doing right now, and I get that. However, working on your grit mindset, taking time to consider where you actually want to go in life and who you want to be, and setting goals to get there will actually help you with everything.

By working through this journal on a regular basis, you will not only develop a grit mindset, but also a better understanding of yourself, which will give you more confidence in everything you do. When you understand how a grit mindset can supercharge your performance, you will succeed. If you learn how to fail, you will be ready and able to face greater challenges.

Writing things down can help you make sense of the complicated world around you. It can also help you make plans and achieve success. I keep a journal to help make sense of the world around me; I make notes, I set goals, I find answers. This is what I want to help you do. This is what I want *My Grit Journal* to be for you – a place and space for you to make sense of the world around you, a place and space for you to celebrate your successes and build on your failures, a place and space for you to learn about yourself and to grow and of course a place and space for you to be you.

HOW KEEPING A GRIT JOURNAL HAS HELPED MY STUDENTS

I have worked with many young people whose success and performance both in school and in their wider lives have been hindered because they had a poor understanding of themselves. They also had an unhealthy attitude to failure – they didn't know how to fail or how to think about how they could improve in the future. These students basically lacked grit – the determination and motivation to make things happen even when faced with a challenge. At the time they didn't realise it, yet through using a journal they soon gained a better understanding of why things were working out a certain way, and gave them the power to change that.

Want to see how it works? Let me introduce you to a few of the students I've helped unlock their potential by using a journal.

When I met her, Mia was a 13-year-old girl who had no sense of who she was. Until I worked with her, she had only ever spoken about herself in negative terms. She really thought she was rubbish at *everything*. She had no confidence in what she could do and so did not see the point of trying. I asked her to start a journal to note down the things she was good at and celebrate her successes. This simple act completely changed her mindset and soon became her new way of thinking. She began to realise that she was not in fact rubbish at everything but successful in a number of areas. Developing this awareness of herself, gave her the strength to tackle and improve on the things she found difficult.

Have you ever spoken in this way, saying you are no good at something? It might be that you think you are rubbish at sport or maths or even writing. Maybe something didn't go so well in the past with that particular thing, or maybe someone said something which made you think negatively. I can remember my Mum saying to me when I was younger, "You're not very good at dancing are you, Kerry?!" This comment had a huge impact on how good I thought I was at dancing and it's lived with me all this time. It has really affected my confidence whenever there is a situation that might involve dancing. The reality is that we all have certain things that we've got hung up about not being good at, and it doesn't do us much good.

Journalling also really helped another student called Josh, who really didn't care much for school. He didn't try as hard as he knew he should. He didn't bother with his homework or revising for his exams – no chance! At 15 years old, he knew that he had to make a change because his exams were just around the corner. His parents were hassling him, his teachers were nagging him – he felt like the whole world was on his back. He had no idea how to turn things around. Reluctantly, he agreed to try journalling to try to bring about change and ultimately exam success. And so the process began with six months to go to his exams.

I encouraged him to write down things he found difficult, both in school and when he played football, every day. We met once a week and went through what he had written down.

When he jotted down his feelings about football, he recalled a time when he had not taken an opportunity to score a goal because he was so worried he would miss it. Josh also wrote about a time when he had not completed his maths homework because he didn't want to get it wrong.

Seeing things in black and white, Josh soon realised that the reason he was underperforming was not because he wasn't capable, but because he often stopped himself trying new things or starting tasks because he was so scared of making a mistake and failing.

This fear of failure was stopping him from succeeding and once Josh 'got' this and realised that it was OK to make mistakes, he was able to take more risks in his learning and his performance immediately accelerated.

WHY, WHEN AND WHERE SHOULD I USE MY GRIT JOURNAL?

My Grit Journal has been designed for you to use once a week to help you plan for the future and chart your success.

As you work through My Grit Journal, you will develop a knowledge and understanding of how you can become more successful and the neuroscience (the science of what's going on in your brain) that promotes and supports this growth. Don't worry, it's a very simple process and an easy to understand philosophy.

Every time you invest your thoughts and ideas in My Grit Journal, you will learn something new about yourself and also about how you personally can achieve success. Everyone is unique, and will discover and aim for different things, but the process is the same for everyone. For some people, this might be developing an understanding of their thinking patterns and how they can change them for the better, for others it might be understanding that it's OK to fail. As you learn more about the theory, there will be tasks for you to complete, which will help you consider who you are and how you can improve either at school, at home or in terms of your friendships.

Within the journal, you will be prompted to think about and identify your successes and failures and plan for the future. It will also encourage you to note key information, so that when you look back through your journal you can see how you've grown and developed. You are constantly changing, so My Grit Journal will give you the opportunity to keep track of key aspects of yourself as you grow.

The key to My Grit Journal is that it is about you for you. There are no right or wrong answers to any of it. It is yours to complete at your leisure when you want to. To achieve optimum success, it is recommended that you use it weekly, but you may find that you want to achieve success sooner and choose to use it every other day or even daily. The Grit Journal is a gradual journey leading you to develop a better understanding of how to become more resilient, set goals and be more successful. Each week, over a period of three months, it introduces you to a new idea and will build on what you have learnt and then it will empower you to use goal-setting as a long-term tool for success. It is a live, working journal to enable you to achieve success and fulfilment.

So, let's do this thing. As you work through your journal, develop grit and become more successful, make sure you share your successes so that others can follow your lead and you can inspire others to do the same.

WEEK 1 ~ ALL ABOUT ME

"SOMETIMES YOU CAN'T SEE YOURSELF CLEARLY UNTIL YOU SEE YOURSELF THROUGH THE EYES OF OTHERS."

Ellen DeGeneres
American comedian, television host, actress, writer and producer

I am important. I am unique.

Quite often in your busy life, you don't have the time or space to think about who you are, what makes you unique and what makes you different to everyone else. You need to have a clear understanding of who you are and what you stand for right now, so that the goals that you set and the plans that you make for your future are right for you and relevant to your hopes and dreams. You can't begin your journey to success if you don't know where you are starting from.

TASK 1: WHO AM I?

This first task can be a tough one. You might never have given any thought as to who you are or what you stand for, so this could be a first for you.

Remember, there is no right or wrong. You cannot fail this. You can share what you do with others or keep it to yourself. Today is your first day of self-exploration.

So, this is your first task.

Draw an image or write a description which symbolises who you are in the box below.

Some things to think about:
What do you look like?
What makes you laugh?
What makes you cry?
What makes you happy?
What makes you angry?

There is no right or wrong; it's all about you, it does not need an explanation!

It could look like this:

Or it could look like this:

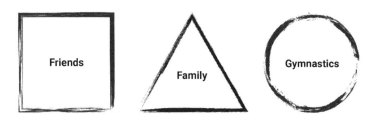

The second one is more abstract than the first. The second one will only make sense to the person who created it and that's absolutely fine. There is no explanation of why this person chose a triangle or circle but it made sense for them. This is what makes My Grit Journal such a unique and empowering experience. In school, in life, you are always expected to explain yourself. When it comes to describing yourself in an abstract way, no explanation is needed.

Now it's time for you to have a go.

TASK 2: WHAT WOULD I LIKE TO CHANGE?

And whilst you're thinking about yourself, let's start thinking about improvement. What is one thing you would like to change about yourself? Write it in the space below:

If you cannot think of anything right now don't worry, you can come back to it later. It is important that you start to think about yourself in terms of both your strengths and weaknesses.

You have crossed the starting line of self-reflection and developing grit. Well done you!

WEEK 2 ~ MINDSET MATTERS

So, last week you considered who you are and what makes you unique. That was a critical self-improvement exercise. If you don't know who you are right now, how can you change and improve? Another thing that can also help as you work towards improvement is considering and charting how well you are doing and why things might not be going as well as hoped. Just identifying something that hasn't gone as well as hoped, can bring about greater success next time.

It can be really tricky to think of things that have gone well if it's not a habit that is well established. Instead, most of us tend to focus on the things that haven't gone as well and end up dwelling on the negative things in our lives. It's time to change that pattern. Let's try it.

TASK 3: HOW ARE THINGS GOING?

List three things that you are proud of this week:

Why you are proud of these things:

What didn't go quite as well as hoped this week:

The key now is being able to reflect and work out why things went wrong so that you can make changes for next time.

Choose one thing from the list above that didn't go as well as you hoped. Why do you think this was? Note your ideas below and try to list as many things as you can think of.

Now, this is the crucial bit.
What could you change to achieve greater success next time? How would you change your attitude, action or mindset so that you improved your performance?

TASK 4: WHAT IS YOUR MINDSET?

Your mindset is what you think, feel and believe about things. It is just as important as how things are going. For instance, you may actually be doing pretty well at something, but you have a poor mindset and think you are terrible at it. This is what grit is all about. It's about understanding how important your mindset is when you are faced with a challenge and being able to overcome any barriers in the way and achieve success. I want to help you cultivate a grit mindset because it will give you the drive and passion to become the best person you can be.

The power of your mindset will have a huge effect on how much effort you put into a task or pursuit and this will have an impact on your performance and success.

In the space below, make notes about the key things you have learnt so far.
What is Mimindset?

What have I learnt about myself?

What would I like to change and get better at? Is it the same as in Week 1 or has your focus for improvement changed?

WEEK 3 ~ MY MINDSET

"WHETHER YOU THINK YOU CAN, OR THINK YOU CAN'T, YOU'RE PROBABLY RIGHT."

Henry Ford
American captain of industry and business magnate

Last week we took a look at what went well, what could have gone better and your mindset. Now we are going to focus on creating a good mindset, as that alone can make the biggest difference in how successful you will be. Dr Carol Dweck is a Professor of Psychology. She says that there are two different types of mindset: a growth mindset and a fixed mindset. If you have a growth mindset, you believe that you can get better at it, and you are very likely to. If you have a fixed mindset you will hold yourself back with the belief that you can't get better at something. You are not either one or the other for everything but, depending what you are doing, one will be more dominant.

According to this theory, learning and intelligence can change. You can grow and get better every day.

TASK 5: WHAT DO I THINK?

Are some people naturally good at some things and not others?

What particular things do you think some people are naturally better at than others?

If some people are naturally good at sport or maths, can anyone get better if they practise?

Quite often, you have a growth mindset in the things that you enjoy and a fixed mindset in the things you don't enjoy. What then happens is that you put more effort and time into the things you have a positive mindset about which makes the gap widen between the things you are good and not so good at.

If you consider your strengths and weaknesses, you can start to see a pattern emerge of how you have different mindsets depending on what you are doing.

TASK 6: WHAT AM I GOOD AND NOT SO GOOD AT?

Think about things that you do every day. Which ones do you think you are good at which ones do you think you are not so good at?

You can use the prompts below to help or add in your own:

	Things I am good at:		Things I am not so good at:
1		1	
2		2	
3		3	
4		4	
5		5	
6		6	
7		7	
8		8	
9		9	
10		10	

Getting up	Cooking	French	Making friends
English	Learning from my mistakes	Helping others	Football
Exercise	PE	Music	Gymnastics
Science	Being proud of my achievements	Forgiving people	Rugby

Being positive	History	Ethics	Reading
Art	Leading people	Being brave	Working hard
Spelling	Geography	Drama	Being kind to myself
Music	Maths	Homework	Keeping friends
Trying new things	Healthy eating	Gaming	Setting goals

One of the reasons why you are much better at some things than others is because you practise them more. This may seem obvious, but some things are such old habits that you may overlook this fact.

Now, look at the things you are good at. I imagine that you spend far more time practising the things that you are good at compared to the things that you are not so good at.

TASK 7: WHY AM I GOOD OR NOT AS GOOD AT THINGS?

Choose your top three things you are good at. Now write why you think you are good at it.

	Things I am good at:		Why I think I am good at this:
1		1	
2		2	
3		3	

Now think about the things you think you are not very good at and note below why you are not very good at it.

	Things I am not so good at:		Why I think I am not good at this:
1		1	
2		2	
3		3	

How you feel and think about something depends on the mindset you have about that certain thing. The more effort you put into something the greater progress you will make. The hardest challenge is when you have to practise something you find difficult. This takes grit.

Now let's try to make a change and start to develop grit. This will not happen by chance, but by setting yourself a plan of action and a goal.

TASK 8: GOAL-SETTING FOR CHANGE

Learning how to set goals and see them through can be difficult because it is tricky to work out what to focus on and how to get there. This was the struggle that one of my students Emily was having. Emily knew that she wanted to get better at maths. She had always found maths difficult, but through her journalling, she realised she had had a fixed mindset about it, thinking she could not possibly get any better. Now she was ready to change that mindset, improve her maths and develop her grit.

The first thing that I needed to find out was exactly what she wanted to change and get better at. After listing all the things she found difficult in maths one thing kept cropping up – fractions. She was ready to start! Emily filled in the first box of the grid on the next page: "I would like to change and get better at fractions". This was a great start.

Now, Emily started to consider how she was going to make this happen. It wasn't going to change just like that. There was no magic wand. We also discussed whether it was up to her parents or teachers to make the change for her, and she agreed that it was not. It was up to her. The only way she was going to make a change and improve was through determined practice in her own time. She explained that she loved gymnastics and spent hours practising at specialist gym classes and at home. I then asked her to think about how much better at fractions she could get if she practised. Her face lit and a huge smile broke – it was a light bulb moment! Emily quickly filled in the next box, How I am going to make this happen: "I am going to practise different fractions questions for 30 minutes, three times a week". This was perfect. Her goal was realistic and achievable. She knew she couldn't do it every night because of other commitments and she wanted to achieve some success. Three evenings a week was certainly do-able.

Then Emily started to think about when she was going to review her progress. As this was her first attempt at setting a goal, she decided that she would initially review her progress after seven days. She wanted to see if she had the grit to succeed and achieve her goal of practising fractions for 30 minutes, three times a week. She was so excited, she couldn't wait to get going. Emily completed the next box, I would like to make this happen: "In the next seven days".

Emily thought long and hard about why she wanted to invest more time into her maths study and wrote "Because I want to improve my performance in maths" in the final box.

That was it, it was that easy. Emily had put everything she needed to in place to make her first change.

Now it's your turn – I want you to be as excited as Emily was when she realised she could make a change for success. Take a look at the things you think you are not so good at and choose one thing you would like to change and improve in the next seven days. Once you have decided what that one thing will be, fill in the grid below.

I would like to change and get better at:	How I am going to make this happen:
I would like to make this happen by this date:	Why I want to make this change:

Next week you will revisit this goal to see how you are doing.

Good luck, you can do this thing, use your grit!

WEEK 4 ~
MY TWO MINDSETS

"MINDSET CHANGE IS NOT ABOUT PICKING UP A FEW POINTERS HERE AND THERE. IT'S ABOUT SEEING THINGS IN A NEW WAY."

Carol Dweck
Professor of Psychology

Last week you took the massive step of setting your first goal. After examining the things that you believed you were and weren't so good at, you focused on an area you would like to make a positive change in. Just like Emily, you decided to make a change and set yourself a date to do it by. This is a huge step towards achieving success and improving your performance.

So how did you do? Let's have a look.

TASK 9: GOAL-SETTING RESULTS

Think back to last week and fill in the grid below:

I would like to change and get better at:	How I am going to make this happen:
I would like to make this happen by this date:	Why I want to make this change:

Goal-setting for change is something you will continue to work on in the coming weeks. Well done for taking this first step towards change! Let's see how a deeper understanding of mindset might help you achieve even more.

Think back to Dr Carol Dweck's two mindsets: fixed mindset or growth mindset.

If you have a growth mindset about something you:	If you have a fixed mindset about something you:
Believe you can learn anything you want to	Believe you are either good at it or not
Persevere when you are frustrated	Give up when you are frustrated
Want to challenge yourself	Don't like to be challenged
Understand that when you fail you learn	Believe that when you fail you are no good
Enjoy being told you are hard-working	Enjoy being told you are smart
Are inspired by those who succeed	Feel threatened if others succeed
Understand that effort and attitude determine everything	Believe abilities determine everything

Now take a look at the list of things from Task 6 in Week 3 that you thought you were good and bad at. So, do you think that the things you are good at are in fact the things you have a growth mindset for and the things you think you are not so good at, those you have a fixed mindset for?

TASK 10: WHAT'S MY MINDSET?

Now, take the list you made in Week 3 of all the things you are good and not good at, now consider that list again and think about which ones you have a fixed mindset in and those you have a growth mindset in.

	I have a growth mindset in these things:		I have a fixed mindset in these things:
1		1	
2		2	
3		3	
4		4	
5		5	
6		6	
7		7	
8		8	
9		9	
10		10	

Now you understand the difference between the two mindsets, let's think in a little bit more in depth about this. Once you are clear about the mindset you are working in you will be able to change the way you think to enhance your performance and success rates.

Think about the things that you have a growth mindset in. I imagine that you believe you can learn and improve when you do those things. You probably enjoy being faced with a new challenge when you do these things and are inspired by others around you when you take part?

This is also the mindset you need to try to develop in the things you find hard or lack confidence in. This will be you developing grit.

TASK 11: GOAL-SETTING WITH A GROWTH MINDSET

Think about one of the things you don't think you're very good at. It can be anything. This will be your focus for change this week. Write down your focus for change here:

For the next seven days, you are going to try to adopt a growth mindset approach through action. To develop a growth mindset, you need to: put in more effort, work harder and practise more. Most importantly, though, you need to really believe you can progress in this.

Document your success below:

The actions I took are as follows:

Day 1

Day 2

Day 3

Day 4

Day 5

Good luck – you can do this thing!

WEEK 5 ~ REFLECTION AND MOVING FORWARD

"IT DOES NOT MATTER HOW SLOWLY YOU GO, SO LONG AS YOU DO NOT STOP."

Confucius
Chinese teacher, editor, politician and philosopher

Last week you looked at developing more of a growth mindset approach to something that you have traditionally found tough and had a negative view towards. Well done for even considering this.

TASK 11: GOAL-SETTING WITH A GROWTH MINDSET — RESULTS

Let's see how you did. Make notes on the following:

What did you want to develop a growth mindset in?

What did you do differently to make this happen?

How successful were you?

Why were you successful or not?

TASK 12: WHAT'S MY PROGRESS?

Well done you, you have completed 25% of this programme of change. Now is the perfect time to recall the amazing change and growth that has already taken place.

Go through each new developmental change and give it tick to show you have achieved and date when you made this great step towards success:

Tick	Goal, Change and Growth	Date
	I know and understand what grit is.	
	I have started to journal the successes in my life.	
	I have a greater understanding of myself, my thoughts and my feelings.	
	I understand that mindset is what motivates me and is the trigger for achieving success.	
	I can explain the difference between a growth mindset and fixed mindset.	
	I can identify the areas in my life where I have a growth and fixed mindset.	
	I have set myself a goal for improvement.	
	I have reflected on the progress towards my goal and whether I have been successful.	

The ability to reflect on your successes and failures is a valuable quality and a trigger for achieving more in life. In your busy life, it is rare that you have the opportunity to think about things that have gone well and things that haven't gone as well as hoped. If you take time to reflect, you can goal-set for future successes.

How have you enjoyed this initial period of change?

Three things that I'm proud of during this time:

Why I am proud of these things:

What hasn't gone quite as well as hoped:

What I would like to focus on in the future:

This is excellent progress. You are developing more grit week by week. You should be very proud. Let's move on.

WEEK 6 ~ PLANNING FOR THE FUTURE

> "ALL OUR DREAMS CAN COME TRUE IF WE
> HAVE THE COURAGE TO PURSUE THEM."

Walt Disney
American entrepreneur, animator, voice actor and film producer

Over the last few weeks, you have got to understand how goal-setting works and what it can help you achieve. To successfully plan for the future, you need to have a really good sense of where you are right now, where you want to be in the future and how you're going to get there.

In the first couple of weeks, you spent time thinking about who you are and what your strengths and weaknesses are. It is now time to think about what your hopes, dreams and aspirations for the future are. Once you get this ball rolling, you can actively work towards planning a successful future for yourself.

TASK 13: WHAT'S MY FUTURE?

I have worked with many adults in the same way that you are working with your journal. Quite often, I hear adults saying that they want to achieve more, they want to be more successful, they want to be happier. They feel stuck and they just don't know how to make things better for themselves.

So I ask them a simple question: What do you want your future to look like? I am always met with a blank look. They have no idea.

If you don't know where you want to get to, how will you be able to make changes and improve to get there?

This issue became apparent with a young person I worked with called Luke. His parents asked me to spend some time mentoring him because they wanted him to spend less time gaming and more time studying at home. Maybe you know someone like Luke. He could see what they were saying, but he lacked the motivation to do anything about it. He started to journal his strengths, weaknesses and focus areas for change. One thing he struggled with was finding a direction for his change, and so I encouraged him to think about the person he wanted to be in the future.

I did the exercise below with Luke, asking him to fill in each box. Luke started by thinking about the things that were important to him at the moment: his friends, his family, his XBox. He also valued going to the gym and walking his dog. He then considered if this would be the same in the future. In 15 years' time, he said he would like to be working as an engineer and still living locally so that he could see his family and go to the gym. He raised his eyebrows as he realised that he was quite happy with where he was at now but just needed to make sure he made plans and choices to ensure he was able to become an engineer if he wanted to.

Happy, friendly and a little bit lazy was how Luke said people would describe him. He was embarrassed about this. Luke went on to say how he admired the adults he knew that seemed to 'work hard' and that he would like to be described as someone who works hard.

So, let's think about the future you want. Note down a few ideas in each of the boxes.

Things that are important to me now:	What I would like to be doing in 15 years' time:
How people might describe me now:	How I would like people to describe me in 15 years' time:

The penny started to drop. It became clear to Luke that whilst he was doing the right thing, he just wasn't putting the effort in, instead he always opted for the easy option.

By considering where you are now and where you want to get to, you are already a step ahead of your peers and many of the adults you know. People spend such a lot of time thinking about what's around the corner, yet they don't really pay attention to what their long-term goals are. By thinking these things through now you will be able to plan for the future.

Now let's look again at what you would like to be doing and how you would like to be described in 15 years' time. What are the three main changes you should make in order to achieve your aspirations?

That is the easy bit. Now note down HOW you are going to do it. Try to be as detailed as you can.

Let's talk about change. Change is Possible, Change is Good.

The theory of growth mindset states that you can change. You can get smarter and improve your performance if you are able to have a growth mindset, which means you can take on challenges and make mistakes.

If you accept that effort and hard work can make you smarter and more successful, you will achieve more and experience greater success. This is how powerful your mindset can be. If you think you can you will and if you think you can't you won't. Using the advice and strategies in this journal, you will be able to change your mindset so that you reach your potential.

TASK 14: WHAT DO I WANT TO CHANGE?

Think about both your academic and personal life. Think about things that you do in and out of school. Now think of your dreams and ambitions.

What do you have to get better at?
What skills do you need to develop?
Where do you need to improve your performance?

Note your ideas below:

These ideas will help focus your goal-setting later on.

WEEK 7 ~ MY ACHIEVEMENTS AND SUCCESSES

"THE THING THAT WE DID WAS, WE DIDN'T GIVE UP"

Jay-Z
American rapper and businessman

Last week you focused on where you want to be in 15 years' time and what you need to do to get there. At the moment, this might all seem beyond your reach and you might be finding it difficult to work out how to get there. Your goals might seem so big that you don't know where to start.

When you feel like this, it is a good idea to remind yourself of things that you have already achieved. These successes probably helped you learn new skills, overcome challenges and cope with failing.

TASK 15: WHAT HAVE I ALREADY ACHIEVED?

Take some time now to remind yourself of the amazing things you have achieved to date. What are you proud of? No matter how big or small, list your achievements and success below:

TASK 16: SMART GOAL-SETTING FOR CHANGE

Now, let's set a goal based on one of the things you would like to change in order to reach your hopes, dreams and aspirations. Be honest. This must be something YOU want – not something your parents, teachers or friends want. You have made huge strides towards success already and now you need to keep up momentum. This change must be something you can achieve in the next seven days.

Whenever we set goals, we must make sure they are SMART. This is an acronym for:

Specific
Measurable
Achievable
Realistic
Time-bound

This will ensure your goal is focused and specific. If you have a very vague goal, it will be hard for you to tell if you have achieved it or not. For example, "I want to spend more time studying" is not specific enough. Instead, using the SMART system it becomes: I will study for one hour on Mondays, Wednesdays and Fridays between 5pm and 6pm for the next two weeks. This goal is measurable because there will be evidence of your study and it is certainly achievable and realistic. Including the time element gives you an end point, as well as an opportunity to review your success and plan a new goal for greater success. For example, if you have been successful and it is going well, you may increase the time of study gradually or include another evening into your schedule.

Have a think, what goal do you want to set for yourself? When you've decided, write it big and bold below:

The change I want to make is:

Now think about how you are going to do this. This has to be specific. So rather than, "try harder in maths" which is hard to measure, instead try "I will practise multiplying fractions for 15 minutes each day". Write it big and bold.

I will make this change by:

Now think about when you going to do this by. Make this short term so that you can regularly chart your progress. Set a time and date and write it big and bold.

I am going to do this by:

Now, remind yourself why you want to make this change. Be honest and again, write it big and bold!

I am doing this because:

Next week we will see how you did. Good luck and if you feel uncertain or doubtful, read through your journal to remind yourself of your changing mindset and grit development.

WEEK 8 ~ FINDING INSPIRATION

> "DON'T LIMIT YOURSELF. MANY PEOPLE LIMIT
> THEMSELVES TO WHAT THEY THINK THEY CAN DO.
> YOU CAN GO AS FAR AS YOUR MIND LETS YOU. WHAT
> YOU BELIEVE, REMEMBER, YOU CAN ACHIEVE."

Mary Kay Ash
American businesswoman

Last week you made your first SMART goal. So how did your goal-setting for change go? Let's see and review your progress:

TASK 17: REVIEWING MY SMART GOAL

The change and improvement I wanted to make was:

I planned to make the change by doing the following:

My successes along the way were:

My fails along the way included:

What I learnt about myself on the way:

My next target for change and improvement is:

This is great stuff – goal-setting, improvement and reflection in action. The more you reflect and the more goals you set, the greater progress you will make. This is so exciting. Well done you!

One of the features of having a growth mindset is being inspired by people around you. So, rather than feeling jealous or threatened by the success of others, people with a growth mindset will be inspired by them. They will want to know how they achieved their success with the aim of doing the same thing themselves.

So, instead of feeling upset that you cannot do something that someone else can you should ask them how they did it. And then you should try to do the same.

TASK 18: WHO DO I ADMIRE?

Think about someone who you know and admire. This could be a friend that is really successful at school or a member of your family who you look up to. You might admire them for their achievements or the way they live their life. It could be that they are generous or kind or spend time helping others or that they are exceptionally good at something. Now, have a go at thinking in a bit more depth about this by answering these questions:

What do you admire about them?

How could you be more like them?

What three questions would you ask them to enable yourself to be more successful?

Now do it. Go on, get in touch with them and ask them. Explain to them that you are trying to be more successful and that they are an inspiration to you. Write down their answers below:

Now think about how their words might help you to achieve your goals.

TASK 19: MY PLEDGE FOR CHANGE

You have already come a long way, but now is the time to make a pledge to really commit to this change you are making. You have already taken huge steps to making positive changes in your life by identifying the change you want to make and setting SMART goals. Now it's the tough bit – maintaining the positive changes you have made. It can be easier to achieve goals in the beginning, because you are fired up with enthusiasm and excitement to make the change. As time goes on, this motivation may wear off and you may find it more difficult to maintain the change. This is where you have to dig down deep and find your grit to keep the momentum going.

— You can do this, I know you can. It's now time to commit to this process by making a pledge for change.

— I understand that if I want to make a change and improve things in my academic, social and personal life it is going to take hard work, practice and grit.

— I will try to focus on small areas of improvement because I understand that small steps can lead to big change.

— I will make sure that the area of my life that I want to change is a realistic and achievable one. Rather than saying, "I want to get better at English" I will be more precise and identify small areas for improvement. For example, "I would like to improve my spelling".

— I understand that to make a change, I will need to dedicate time to practising this skill. For example, if I want to improve my spelling I will set aside time to learn three new spellings each day.

— I know that I may fail when I try to make a change. Instead of giving up, I will use my grit and growth mindset to reflect and set new goals.

— By adopting a growth mindset, I will make small changes which will result in greater success in all areas of my life.

Signed: _____

Date: _____

You should be very proud of the commitment you are making to become the best you can. Your change in mindset is remarkable and you should see your commitment to growth having an impact on all areas of your life.

Next week, you will have the opportunity to focus on your progress by reflecting on your achievements and planning your continued journey towards success.

WEEK 9 ~ REFLECTION AND MOVING FORWARD

This is amazing. You have now been working to improve yourself for two months. This is remarkable commitment and dedication. Well, done you! Let's see how far you have come in the last month.

TASK 20: REVIEWING MY SECOND MONTH

As you did in Task 12, go through each new developmental change and give it tick to show you have achieved it and the date when you took this great step towards success:

Tick	Goal, Change and Growth	Date
	I have considered my hopes, dreams and ambitions for the future.	
	I have a greater sense of what I need to do to achieve my long-term goals.	
	I know what I need to develop in order to be successful.	
	I have celebrated my successes and all that I am proud of.	
	I have set myself a goal for improvement.	
	I understand that for continued improvement I need to be setting and reviewing my goals regularly.	
	I am inspired by people around me and understand the importance of learning from them.	
	I have made a pledge to continue this journey of growth and improvement.	

How have you enjoyed this period of change?
Answer the questions below:

These are three things I have done in the last month that I am proud of:

Why I am proud of these things:

What hasn't gone quite as well as hoped in the last month:

What I would like to focus on in the future:

You have already made great progress and should be proud of how far you've come. An understanding of how our brain works and the learning process will also help you achieve even more. Next week you will learn about neuroplasticity – a fascinating concept which will open your eyes to how much you could actually achieve.

WEEK 10 ~ NEURODLASTICITY IN ACTION

"PICTURE YOUR BRAIN FORMING NEW CONNECTIONS AS YOU MEET THE CHALLENGE AND LEARN. KEEP ON GOING."

Carol Dweck
Professor of Psychology

By now you have a good understanding of mindset and how to set goals, but having a better understanding of how your brain works can supercharge your progress. I often hear young people say that they cannot do or understand things because they are 'stupid' or thick' yet once they realise that the reason they are unable to do something is because of the way their brain is wired, it gives them the grit to try and therefore succeed.

For example, I once taught a boy called Max who said that he was no good at algebra. To him this was fact. He felt there was no point trying because he had the fixed mindset that you were either good at things or not, and he most definitely was no good when it came to algebra. Max was one of the toughest kids in the school and changing his mind about anything was not an easy thing to do. I asked him if he would give me 10 minutes to explain the neuroscience behind learning with the aim of showing him that he was not stupid. He reluctantly agreed. This is what I taught him.

I explained to him that his brain is the most powerful thing in the world and it works just like a muscle. As with all the other muscles in our body we have to exercise it to keep it strong and work hard to develop it to make us smarter. I went on and explained that our brain weighs about 1 kilogram and is made up mostly of water and about 10% fat. This fact was met with a squirm from Max, but he was keen that I carried on. I explained that whilst our brain is about 2% of our body's weight, it actually uses 20% of our body's energy to perform miraculous things every single nanosecond. These miraculous things are powered by the neurons in our brain. I told Max that his brain is made up of about 1 billion neurons and these "messenger" cells are responsible for carrying information around our brain.

I stopped and paused in my explanation. He was hooked, he hadn't learnt anything about his brain before.

I carried on. I told him that the role of neurons or "messenger" cells in our brain is to make us smarter. They travel along around 10,000 neural connections or pathways, which is how information is transmitted around our body. As the information is passed along the neural pathways we can think, act and feel.

If we are used to doing something and have practised it many times, the neural pathway works well as it has been well travelled by the "messenger" cells, and this is what makes us good at something. When we try something new or difficult we have to create a new neural pathway which is harder for the "messenger" cells to travel across. But the more the "messenger" cells go across that pathway, the easier it becomes for them to do so, meaning it's easier for the information they carry to get from one place to another.

If we never create or strengthen these new paths we can't grow or improve. The more we practise, the more this new thing we have learnt becomes a habit. This is neuroplasticity in action. This is your brain growing. This is you getting smarter. "Neuro" means brain and "plasticity" means change. You can literally change your brain like moulding Plasticine.

I stopped there and Max's mouth was open all agog. "Why has no one told me this before?" he exclaimed, "You mean that for all these years since Year 2 I thought the reason I found maths tough is because I'm thick but it's not that. It's because my neural pathway is not quite big or smooth enough?" "Yes," I replied. "And if I practise the really tough stuff I will create new pathways and become smarter at maths?" "Yes," I replied.

Max had had the light bulb moment. He understood that when he tries something new or tries to change the way he acts, thinks or feels it is hard at the beginning because the neural pathway isn't established. Rather, than give up like he used to, he now knows that as he practises and uses his grit, his neural pathways will become established and make whatever he is trying to do easier. I had to make it very clear to him that learning something new, changing the way we act, think or feel about something might take a time and so it is important to remind himself of how neuroplasticity works.

He agreed to face new challenges and things he found hard with a renewed grit as he now understood that through practice and hard work he would master what he was trying to achieve.

With that, he stood up and left. Little did I know that he went straight to the Head Teacher's office to ask why he hadn't been taught this before and that all students should know this. He argued, "If everyone knew how neuroplasticity worked, they would understand that they find things hard because the pathways are not there yet, not because they are thick."

So, this is neuroplasticity. The fact that when you try new things or find something hard, it is not because you are not smart enough, it is because the neural pathway has not yet travelled enough for this new information to flow along. With determination, practice and grit you can create new neural pathways for information to pass along more easily.

TASK 21: WHAT IS HAPPENING INSIDE MY BRAIN

In your own words, describe what neuroplasticity is and how it works:

Who do you know that would benefit from learning about neuroplasticity? Is there someone you know who thinks they cannot change or get better at something?

Why do you think they would benefit from learning about neuroplasticity?

In which areas of your personal, social and academic life do you need to strengthen your neural pathways?

TASK 22: STRENGTHENING MY NEURAL PATHWAYS

Now let's use this new knowledge to set some more goals.

Set yourself a goal below:
This week I intend to strengthen my neural pathway in the following area:

I will achieve this by doing the following: (Top tip – make sure your answer includes practice to create or strengthen your neural pathways!)

I will know if I've been successful because:

You are getting grittier week by week, and you should be very proud of your hard work and effort. The reflection and goal-setting you are engaging with can only bring success. The problem can be when things go wrong. This can knock our confidence and motivation. Let's see how failing and making mistakes is a critical part of learning.

WEEK 11 ~ THE ART OF FAILING

> "SUCCESS IS WALKING FROM FAILURE TO FAILURE WITH NO LOSS OF ENTHUSIASM."
>
> **Winston Churchill**
> **British Prime Minister, army officer and writer**

You are now in the habit of setting yourself goals and striving to improve, many people struggle with this because they have a fear of failing. A fear of failing is when you stop yourself doing or trying something just in case you get it wrong or make a mistake. Instead, you only invest your time and effort in things which you find easy and are good at. If you have a fear of failing you may find it difficult to try new things, face a challenge or even attempt a test. Whatever it is, you need to learn how to fail well in order to make the most progress.

It is important to note that people are often prevented from even starting a task because of their fear of failing. I have seen young people literally freeze in test situations because they are scared of failing. I've seen some never try to learn a new skill because they don't want to mess up and look silly in front of their peers. The fact that a fear of failure can prevent people from trying new things, taking on a challenge or completing a task will have a huge impact on how successful they are.

You might think that if you fail or make a mistake:

— People will laugh at you
— You will no longer be the best
— The experience can only be negative

This is a fixed mindset approach, which stops you making as much progress as you should because you are scared of failing. Professor Carol Dweck says:

In the fixed mindset, everything is about the outcome. If you fail — or if you're not the best — it's all been wasted. The growth mindset allows people to value what they're doing regardless of the outcome.

This can happen in all areas of your life. I know students who do not complete homework because they fear getting it wrong. There are adults who don't apply for jobs because they are scared of failing to get an interview and academics who are unable to bring themselves to attempt a challenging task through fear of getting it wrong. This fear can strike anyone, and ultimately prevents people from achieving success, making progress and reaching their potential. If we are able to recognise that it is our fear that is stopping us achieving, not our ability or talent, we can seek to address it.

TASK 23: MY FEARS

When have you been scared or worried about failing, getting it wrong or making a mistake? I can think of at least five for myself straight away! Have a think and then write down some of your biggest fails below. Be honest, no one will know!

To experience ultimate progress and success, you need to learn how to make good mistakes and fail well. This is how you will move forward. When I teach children, I explain to them that they should never achieve 10 out of 10 in the tasks that I give them. This goes against everything they believe in. In their eyes, they want to get full marks for everything they do. I then explain to them that if they get 100% they will never learn anything. What sort of teacher am I if they know all the answers already? I need to teach them something new and they need to find their own challenges in life. That is when progress happens. This is developing grit.

The key is being to reflect and goal-set when you fail or make a mistake. For every mistake you make, you must consider what went wrong, create a new plan for next time and then try again.

The only time you fail is when you stop trying.

FAMOUS FAILURES

"I have failed on an epic scale. An exceptionally short-lived marriage had imploded and I was jobless, a lone parent, and as poor as it is possible to be in modern Britain, without being homeless. The fears that my parents had had for me, and that I had had for myself, had both come to pass, and by every usual standard, I was the biggest failure I knew."

JK Rowling
British novelist, screenwriter and producer

"I didn't see it then, but it turned out that getting fired from Apple was the best thing that could've happened to me."

Steve Jobs
American entrepreneur and business magnate

"I've probably earned the right to screw up a few times. I don't want the fear of failure to stop me from doing what I really care about."

Emma Watson
British actress, model and activist

"It's fine to celebrate success but it is more important to heed the lessons of failure."

Bill Gates
American business magnate, investor, author, philanthropist, humanitarian and principal founder of Microsoft Corporation

"Failure is a great teacher, and if you are open to it, every mistake has a lesson to offer."

Oprah Winfrey
American media proprietor, talk show host, actress, produce and philanthropist

TASK 24: LEARNING FROM FAILURE

No one really likes to fail, but if you adopt a growth mindset towards failing you will experience more success than if you stopped yourself from trying or doing something because you are scared of getting it wrong or making a mistake. This takes grit.

Everyone fails in life. It is how we respond to failure that is the key to success. When we fail, we learn. This is the only response to success.

We learn by considering why we failed. We need to answer these questions:

— What was the failure?
— Why did I fail?
— What can I do next time to generate more success?

Through this process of reflection, we can goal-set for progress and future success. Now reflect on something that you failed at and describe it below:

What I failed at:

Why I failed:

What I could do next time to generate more success.

Despite all your hard work and your willingness to fail, there might still be something that is not progressing as well as you hoped. Don't give up, find your grit and it's time to consider the ultimate power of yet.

WEEK 12 ~
THE POWER OF YET

> "WE LIKE TO THINK OF OUR CHAMPIONS AND IDOLS AS SUPERHEROES WHO WERE BORN DIFFERENT FROM US. WE DON'T LIKE TO THINK OF THEM AS RELATIVELY ORDINARY PEOPLE WHO MADE THEMSELVES EXTRAORDINARY."

Carol Dweck
Professor of Psychology

Now you've got the right attitude towards failure, I want to introduce you to something that the psychologist Carol Dweck associated with a growth mindset – the power of yet.

When you find things tough or you hit a brick wall, the easiest thing to do is to give up. If there is a chance that things might not turn out as planned or there is a greater than usual element of risk, you might be tempted to not try as hard you could or should.

In situations such as this, instead of saying 'I can't' do something, Carol Dweck suggests adding the simple notion of 'yet'. If we add 'yet' to the end, 'I can't do something yet', it means you are not finished. It's that simple. So, for example, if you say, 'I can't do algebra," you are in a fixed mindset. There is no moving forward. You think that your intelligence and progress are fixed, and that there is nothing you can do about it.

Now put 'yet' after it. "I can't do algebra yet." This indicates that learning is a process and there is further room for growth. It adds the element that you understand that your brain is continually growing through hard work and making mistakes. It shows that you understand neuroplasticity. It shows that you have grit.

Adding this simple and new dimension to your learning and everyday challenges will add a different perspective – one which enables growth and success.

TASK 25: WHAT CAN'T I DO YET?

Have a think about the things that you cannot do or find tricky. List them below:

	Things I can't do or find difficult:
1	I can't …
2	I can't …
3	I can't …
4	I can't …
5	I can't …

Now add the growth concept of 'yet':

	Things I can't do or find difficult:	
1	I can't …	…. YET
2	I can't …	…. YET
3	I can't …	…. YET
4	I can't …	…. YET
5	I can't …	…. YET

You have now added the concept of growth and change to your mindset. Your intelligence is not fixed and your accomplishments can grow through hard work, making mistakes and setting goals. This can all be supported by using the power of yet to guide you in all that you do.

Where and when would you benefit from using the power of yet?

TASK 26: HOW CAN I HELP OTHERS?

Now you have a good understanding of growth mindset theory and are developing grit, you might be able to identify friends and family who are stuck in a fixed mindset.

The only time you fail is when you stop trying. Who do you think would benefit from understanding this? Name the people below who you are going to share this knowledge with:

You know that if you are stuck in a fixed mindset you will not reach your potential and the success that is deserved.
How could you help someone stuck in a fixed mindset?

What do you think are the three most important aspects of having a growth mindset?

What advice would you give to someone who thinks, 'I can't do it'?

You have made such great progress you can now inspire others to do the same. Do it now. Don't waste any time. Help others achieve their potential and beyond.

WEEK 13 ~ REFLECTION AND MOVING FORWARD

> "IT IS NOT THE STRONGEST OF THE SPECIES THAT SURVIVE, NOR THE MOST INTELLIGENT, BUT THE ONE MOST RESPONSIVE TO CHANGE."

Charles Darwin
English naturalist, geologist and biologist

This is impressive. You have now been working to improve yourself for three months. This is fantastic commitment and dedication. Well, done you!

TASK 27: REVIEWING THE GRIT PROCESS

Let's see how far you have come in the last month. As you did in Task 12 and 20, go through each new developmental change and give it a tick to show you have achieved it and the date when you took this great step towards success:

Tick	Goal, Change and Growth	Date
	I have a better understanding of how my brain works and neuroplasticity.	
	I now understand that it's OK to fail and it is this that leads to greater growth and success.	
	I will use and promote the power of yet.	
	As someone who works in a growth mindset, I understand that I have the capacity and skills to inspire and help others achieve more.	
	I have developed grit.	

TASK 28: TIME TO REFLECT

As you have used this journal, you have developed the essential skill of reflection. This is a skill that will be very useful to you in all aspects of your life. At this point, you should be in the habit of continuously reflecting on your academic, social and personal life. It is important to reflect and think about your successes and failures so that you can goal-set for improvement. This is crucial if you want to get better and to make sure you reach your potential.

Think about your last seven days. What things have you been proud of this week and why are you proud of them? Think about the hard work you invested in the things you are proud of and the grit you demonstrated. Note your ideas below:

Is there anything you would change or improve next time?

Now think about the things that didn't go as well as planned in the last seven weeks. Why didn't they go as well as you hoped? Make some notes below:

What would you change and improve next time?

YOU ARE AMAZING!

You have achieved so much in such a short space of time. The next step is for you to set goals and achieve success on your own regularly. In the following pages, you will find a space to set your goals, a log for you to note all your successes so that you have a visual reminder of how far you have come as well as prompts to continue your path of success and achievement. You can set your own goals, at your own pace, and review your successes and failures regularly. This is you using your grit. This is you making positive changes and progress.

The next section is for you to plan and goal-set for the future. You can do this either daily, weekly or monthly – there are no set rules but whatever fits in with your hopes, dreams and aspirations. Whilst the goal-setting is important, you must make sure that you also reflect on your success to identify where things went wrong and how it could be better next time.

"YOU MUST BE
THE CHANGE YOU WISH
TO SEE IN THE WORLD."

Gandhi
Indian activist

GOAL-SETTING FOR CHANGE

This is the exciting bit.

This is when you will really grow and achieve more success.

This is your future!

Now, this is where you are going to see the real change taking place. You have all the tools, skills and strategies to make positive changes wherever and whenever you want. Remember, your grit will enable you to achieve your goals, and if it doesn't work out the first time you know how to reflect, review and goal-set again.

You are now ready to start this journey on your own. In the following months, you will set yourself achievable goals which, when you meet them, will rocket your success beyond recognition. You now have the inner drive and grit to achieve this on your own, without your parents and without your teachers.

If, at any point, you feel as though you are lacking the motivation and drive to improve, re-read the journal and look back on what you have achieved so far. Remind yourself of how and why mindset matters, and think about whether or not you are working in a fixed mindset or growth mindset. You can also take another look at the section on neuroplasticity and revisit the idea that your brain is always growing, it is malleable and can change and adapt through hard work and practice. If you find that fear of failure has crept up on you again, go back and retrain your brain to understand that failing is an important part of learning.

You can do this – you've got this far and made huge progress to date, so now is the time to keep going. The initial change in mindset can be the easy part, it's maintaining that grit and drive that can be the challenge.

In the rest of this journal, you will find easy goal-setting exercises that will help you maintain your current drive for improvement. Each month, have a think about both your academic and personal life. Think about things that you do in and out of school. Then think of your dreams and ambitions and ask yourself the following questions:

What would you like to get better at?
What skills do you need to develop?
Where do you need to improve your performance?

And then set yourself a goal – a SMART goal for the month. At the end of the month, I want you to re-read your goal, review how you did and celebrate your success. Then set yourself your next goal for the next month.

Just imagine how successful you could be in 12 months' time – this is so exciting! Ready to set the goal for month one?

GOAL-SETTING FOR SUCCESS

MONTH ONE

So, this is the first goal you are going to set and see through on your own. You have to carefully consider exactly what you want to get better at. What is important to you right now? Write your first goal big and bold below:

I am going to:

Great stuff. Now, thinking about what you've learnt about goal-setting, let's make sure it's SMART:

Is your goal specific?	Yes/No	Explain how is it specific?	
Is your goal measurable?	Yes/No	How can you measure it?	
Is your goal achievable?	Yes/No	How do you know this?	
Is your goal realistic?	Yes/No	How can you tell?	
Is your goal within a timeframe of this month?	Yes/No	Can you do this in one month?	

If you've amended your goal to make it SMART, write your smarter goal below:

I am going to:

Now sign below to commit to your goal, write today's date and when you are going to review it:

Signed:

Today's date:

To be reviewed on this date: (put one month's time)

REFLECT, REVIEW, GOAL-SET

MONTH ONE

So, how did you do? Let's make a few notes below:

What did you find easy about working towards your goal?

What did you find difficult?

When you found things difficult, how did thinking about your grit factor and growth mindset help?

What would you do differently next time?

What are you most proud of in the last month?

So, to summarise, last month you set yourself a goal for self-improvement using the grit you have developed. Now, let's see how you did. Fill in the following:

My goal in the last month was to:

I achieved my goal because:

I did not achieve my goal because:

What have I learnt about myself, my grit and my mindset in the last month:

My mission next month is to improve my performance and success in the following area:

Well done! You have successfully set yourself a goal, reflected and reviewed your performance. This is a huge achievement – one which you should be very proud of!

Now to keep going – let's move forward and set another goal for next month!

GOAL-SETTING FOR SUCCESS

MONTH TWO

So, you have successfully used your grit to set, reflect and review your first goal. Well done. Now let's set another goal. What would you like to improve next? Maybe focus on your performance at school or you may already have a clear idea what you want to achieve.

Write your goal big and bold below:

Great stuff. Now, thinking about what you've learnt about goal-setting, let's make sure it's SMART:

Is your goal specific?	Yes/No	Explain how is it specific?	
Is your goal measurable?	Yes/No	How can you measure it?	
Is your goal achievable?	Yes/No	How do you know this?	
Is your goal realistic?	Yes/No	How can you tell?	
Is your goal within a timeframe of this month?	Yes/No	Can you do this in one month?	

If you've amended your goal to make it SMART, write your smarter goal below:

I am going to:

Now sign below to commit to your goal, write today's date and when you are going to review it:

Signed:

Today's date:

To be reviewed on this date: (put one month's time)

REFLECT, REVIEW, GOAL-SET

MONTH TWO

So, how did you do? Let's make a few notes below:

What did you find easy about working towards your goal?

What did you find difficult?

When you found things difficult, how did thinking about your grit factor and growth mindset help?

What would you do differently next time?

What are you most proud of in the last month?

So, to summarise, last month you set yourself a goal for self-improvement using the grit you have developed. Now, let's see how you did. Fill in the following:

My goal in the last month was to:

I achieved my goal because:

I did not achieve my goal because:

What have I learnt about myself, my grit and my mindset in the last month:

My mission next month is to improve my performance and success in the following area:

Excellent stuff! You are an absolute star. Onwards and upwards.

GOAL-SETTING FOR SUCCESS

MONTH THREE

Well done for last month's achievement. Remember, if you find an aspect of your drive to improve difficult, read back over the difference between fixed and growth mindsets to remind yourself of why you might be finding it hard. If you are still trying, you haven't failed – this is the power of yet!

Let's set another goal. Why not focus on a goal related to your health this month – maybe you could look at your diet, sleep or exercise regime. What would you like to improve?

Write your goal big and bold below:

Great stuff. Now, thinking about what you've learnt about goal-setting, let's make sure it's SMART:

Is your goal specific?	Yes/No	Explain how is it specific?	
Is your goal measurable?	Yes/No	How can you measure it?	
Is your goal achievable?	Yes/No	How do you know this?	
Is your goal realistic?	Yes/No	How can you tell?	
Is your goal within a timeframe of this month?	Yes/No	Can you do this in one month?	

If you've amended your goal to make it SMART, write your smarter goal below:

I am going to:

Now sign below to commit to your goal, write today's date and when you are going to review it:

Signed:

Today's date:

To be reviewed on this date: (put one month's time)

REFLECT, REVIEW, GOAL-SET

MONTH THREE

So, how did you do? Let's make a few notes below:

What did you find easy about working towards your goal?

What did you find difficult?

When you found things difficult, how did thinking about your grit factor and mindset help?

What would you do differently next time?

What are you most proud of in the last month?

So, to summarise, last month you set yourself a goal for self-improvement using the grit you have developed. Now, let's see how you did.

My goal in the last month was to:

I achieved my goal because:

I did not achieve my goal because:

What I have learnt about myself, my grit and my mindset in the last month:

My mission next month is to improve my performance and success in the following area:

Excellent! That's three months of improvement under your belt already. Let's move on.

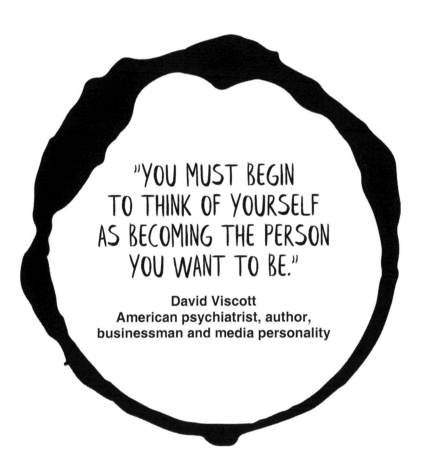

"YOU MUST BEGIN
TO THINK OF YOURSELF
AS BECOMING THE PERSON
YOU WANT TO BE."

David Viscott
American psychiatrist, author,
businessman and media personality

GOAL-SETTING FOR SUCCESS

MONTH FOUR

Wow, you've already done three months of goal-setting, so congratulations. Maybe this month you could think about something you would like to do less of to help improve yourself. Maybe watch less Netflix, or reduce the amount of time you spend gaming, or limit the amount of time you spend on social media. You may already have a good idea of what you would like to change. So let's go.

Write your goal below:

Excellent! So, is your goal SMART?

Is your goal specific?	Yes/No	Explain how is it specific?	
Is your goal measurable?	Yes/No	How can you measure it?	
Is your goal achievable?	Yes/No	How do you know this?	
Is your goal realistic?	Yes/No	How can you tell?	
Is your goal within a timeframe of this month?	Yes/No	Can you do this in one month?	

If you've amended your goal to make it SMART, write your smarter goal below:

Now sign below to commit to your goal, write today's date and when you are going to review it:

Signed:

Today's date:

To be reviewed on this date: (put one month's time)

REFLECT, REVIEW, GOAL-SET

MONTH FOUR

So, how did you do? Let's make a few notes below:

What did you find easy about working towards your goal?

What did you find difficult?

When you found things difficult, how did thinking about your grit factor and mindset help?

What would you do differently next time?

What are you most proud of in the last month?

So, to summarise, last month you set yourself a goal for self-improvement using the grit you have developed. Now, let's see how you did.

My goal in the last month was to:

I achieved my goal because:

I did not achieve my goal because:

What I have learnt about myself, my grit and my mindset in the last month:

My mission next month is to improve my performance and success in the following area:

Fantastic! Let's move forward and embrace the challenges that month 5 might offer you.

GOAL-SETTING FOR SUCCESS

MONTH FIVE

So, you've achieved four goals so far using your grit and everything you've learnt about mindset, now it's time for you to set your fifth monthly goal. I'm sure you have a clear idea about what you would like to focus on but if not, how about looking at your relationships? This could be with your friends or someone in your family. You might want to be kinder or spend more time with them. Have a think and then write your goal below:

Now to make sure your goal is SMART:

Is your goal specific?	Yes/No	Explain how is it specific?	
Is your goal measurable?	Yes/No	How can you measure it?	
Is your goal achievable?	Yes/No	How do you know this?	
Is your goal realistic?	Yes/No	How can you tell?	
Is your goal within a timeframe of this month?	Yes/No	Can you do this in one month?	

If you've amended your goal to make it SMART, write your smarter goal below:

Now sign below to commit to your goal, write today's date and when you are going to review it:

Signed:

Today's date:

To be reviewed on this date: (put one month's time)

REFLECT, REVIEW, GOAL-SET

MONTH FIVE

So, how did you do? Let's make a few notes below:

What did you find easy about working towards your goal?

What did you find difficult?

When you found things difficult, how did thinking about your grit factor and mindset help?

What would you do differently next time?

What are you most proud of in the last month?

So, to summarise, last month you set yourself a goal for self-improvement using the grit you have developed. Now, let's see how you did.

My goal in the last month was to:

I achieved my goal because:

I did not achieve my goal because:

What I have learnt about myself, my grit and my mindset in the last month:

My mission next month is to improve my performance and success in the following area:

Another goal in the bag! Now to keep going – let's move forward and set another goal!

GOAL-SETTING FOR SUCCESS

MONTH SIX

Well done. You've been goal-setting for nearly six months now, which is such an achievement. Now you can build on your success and achieve even more. If you are not clear which goal to set this month, have a look back through your previous goals. Maybe revisit a previous goal and set yourself a greater challenge for even more improvement in a particular area. Now that you are in the habit of setting goals and improving, you'll be able to push yourself even more.

Write your goal below:

Is it SMART? Double check below:

Is your goal specific?	Yes/No	Explain how is it specific?	
Is your goal measurable?	Yes/No	How can you measure it?	
Is your goal achievable?	Yes/No	How do you know this?	
Is your goal realistic?	Yes/No	How can you tell?	
Is your goal within a timeframe of this month?	Yes/No	Can you do this in one month?	

If you've amended your goal to make it SMART, write your smarter goal below:

Now sign below to commit to your goal and write today's date and when you are going to review it:

Signed:

Today's date:

To be reviewed: (put one month's time)

REFLECT, REVIEW, GOAL-SET

MONTH SIX

So, how did you do? Let's make a few notes below:

What did you find easy about working towards your goal?

What did you find difficult?

When you found things difficult, how did thinking about your grit factor and mindset help?

What would you do differently next time?

What are you most proud of in the last month?

So, to summarise, last month you set yourself a goal for self-improvement using the grit you have developed. Now, let's see how you did.

My goal in the last month was to:

I achieved my goal because:

I did not achieve my goal because:

What I have learnt about myself, my grit and my mindset in the last month:

My mission next month is to improve my performance and success in the following area:

This is phenomenal – half a year of setting goals, half a year of challenging yourself, half a year of pure grit!

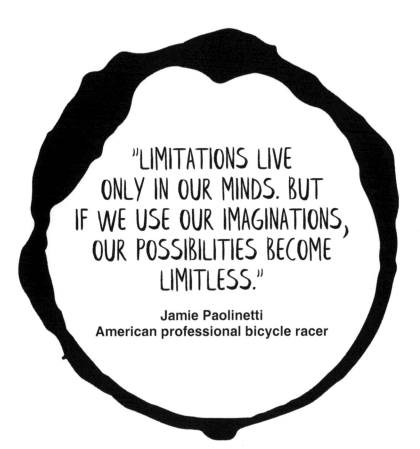

"LIMITATIONS LIVE ONLY IN OUR MINDS. BUT IF WE USE OUR IMAGINATIONS, OUR POSSIBILITIES BECOME LIMITLESS."

Jamie Paolinetti
American professional bicycle racer

GOAL-SETTING FOR SUCCESS

MONTH SEVEN

You have achieved so much in such a short space of time. Think about all the things you have accomplished in the last six months. Note down the successes you are most proud of below:

That is just amazing! So what are you going to focus on in the next sixth months? Think about your strengths and weaknesses – what would you like to improve? To start with, let's set a goal for month seven.

Write your goal below:

Is it SMART?

Is your goal specific?	Yes/No	Explain how is it specific?	
Is your goal measurable?	Yes/No	How can you measure it?	
Is your goal achievable?	Yes/No	How do you know this?	
Is your goal realistic?	Yes/No	How can you tell?	
Is your goal within a timeframe of this month?	Yes/No	Can you do this in one month?	

If you've amended your goal to make it SMART, write your smarter goal below:

Now sign below to commit to your goal and write today's date and when you are going to review it:

Signed:

Today's date:

To be reviewed: (put one month's time)

REFLECT, REVIEW, GOAL-SET

MONTH SEVEN

So, how did you do? Let's make a few notes below:

What did you find easy about working towards your goal?

What did you find difficult?

When you found things difficult, how did thinking about your grit factor and mindset help?

What would you do differently next time?

What are you most proud of in the last month?

So, to summarise, last month you set yourself a goal for self-improvement using the grit you have developed. Now, let's see how you did.

My goal in the last month was to:

I achieved my goal because:

I did not achieve my goal because:

What I have learnt about myself, my grit and my mindset in the last month:

My mission next month is to improve my performance and success in the following area:

This is great – because of your grit, goal-setting for success is now becoming part of your lifestyle. This can only mean one thing: that you are on the right path to reach your potential!

GOAL-SETTING FOR SUCCESS

MONTH EIGHT

So you are now into month eight. What are you going to focus on this month? If you are unsure, how about thinking about your education. Maybe you could spend more time on your homework or extend your learning by reading more about a subject in your own time. Go on, you can do it!

Write your goal below:

You should be an expert at this by now; is it SMART?

Is your goal specific?	Yes/No	Explain how is it specific?	
Is your goal measurable?	Yes/No	How can you measure it?	
Is your goal achievable?	Yes/No	How do you know this?	
Is your goal realistic?	Yes/No	How can you tell?	
Is your goal within a timeframe of this month?	Yes/No	Can you do this in one month?	

If you've amended your goal to make it SMART, write your smarter goal below:

Now sign below to commit to your goal and write today's date and when you are going to review it:

Signed:

Today's date:

To be reviewed: (put one month's time)

REFLECT, REVIEW, GOAL-SET

MONTH EIGHT

So, how did you do? Let's make a few notes below:

What did you find easy about working towards your goal?

What did you find difficult?

When you found things difficult, how did thinking about your grit factor and mindset help?

What would you do differently next time?

What are you most proud of in the last month?

So, to summarise, last month you set yourself a goal for self-improvement using the grit you have developed. Now, let's see how you did.

My goal in the last month was to:

I achieved my goal because:

I did not achieve my goal because:

What I have learnt about myself, my grit and my mindset in the last month:

My mission next month is to improve my performance and success in the following area:

Excellent – I hope that you were successful but if not, you must remember that it's OK to fail and as long as you keep trying you will definitely make progress.

GOAL-SETTING FOR SUCCESS

MONTH NINE

So this is a freestyle month, which means your goal this month can be a little different; sometimes the thing that you need to improve on may surprise you somewhat. It could be your manners, or being more helpful at home, or it could even be your punctuality, your organisation or communication skills. Think about your whole life, and think about the smaller elements that you'd like to improve, both for your own benefit and the benefit of those around you. Whatever it is, write your goal below:

Nice one. So is it SMART?

Is your goal specific?	Yes/No	Explain how is it specific?	
Is your goal measurable?	Yes/No	How can you measure it?	
Is your goal achievable?	Yes/No	How do you know this?	
Is your goal realistic?	Yes/No	How can you tell?	
Is your goal within a timeframe of this month?	Yes/No	Can you do this in one month?	

If you've amended your goal to make it SMART, write your smarter goal below:

Now sign below to commit to your goal and write today's date and when you are going to review it:

Signed:

Today's date:

To be reviewed: (put one month's time)

REFLECT, REVIEW, GOAL-SET

MONTH NINE

So, how did you do? Let's make a few notes below:

What did you find easy about working towards your goal?

What did you find difficult?

When you found things difficult, how did thinking about your grit factor and mindset help?

What would you do differently next time?

What are you most proud of in the last month?

So, to summarise, last month you set yourself a goal for self-improvement using the grit you have developed. Now, let's see how you did.

My goal in the last month was to:

I achieved my goal because:

I did not achieve my goal because:

What I have learnt about myself, my grit and my mindset in the last month:

My mission next month is to improve my performance and success in the following area:

I'm glad you enjoyed your freestyle month and I hope you have managed to make a positive change to an aspect of your life. Let's sprint on to month ten.

"THERE ARE NO
SHORTCUTS TO ANY
PLACE WORTH GOING."

Helen Keller
American author, political
activist and lecturer

GOAL-SETTING FOR SUCCESS

MONTH TEN

You really do have the grit factor. To keep goal-setting for this long with the amount of enthusiasm you have takes a great deal of hard work and effort. Well done you.

What are you going to focus on this month? How about looking at your health again? Could your diet be better to enable you to learn more effectively? Maybe doing a bit more exercise might help you to relax and sleep better? Or how about drinking more water to keep your brain hydrated? What could you improve to help you reach your potential?

Note your goal below:

Check that it's SMART below:

Is your goal specific?	Yes/No	Explain how is it specific?	
Is your goal measurable?	Yes/No	How can you measure it?	
Is your goal achievable?	Yes/No	How do you know this?	
Is your goal realistic?	Yes/No	How can you tell?	
Is your goal within a timeframe of this month?	Yes/No	Can you do this in one month?	

If you've amended your goal to make it SMART, write your smarter goal below:

Now sign below to commit to your goal and write today's date and when you are going to review it:

Signed:

Today's date:

To be reviewed: (put one month's time)

REFLECT, REVIEW, GOAL-SET

MONTH TEN

So, how did you do? Let's make a few notes below:

What did you find easy about working towards your goal?

What did you find difficult?

When you found things difficult, how did thinking about your grit factor and mindset help?

What would you do differently next time?

What are you most proud of in the last month?

So, to summarise, last month you set yourself a goal for self-improvement using the grit you have developed. Now, let's see how you did.

My goal in the last month was to:

I achieved my goal because:

I did not achieve my goal because:

What I have learnt about myself, my grit and my mindset in the last month:

My mission next month is to improve my performance and success in the following area:

This is amazing. You must be so proud of yourself. I really hope you are, and that you are sharing all of the positive changes you are making with your friends and family. They will certainly be inspired by you!

GOAL-SETTING FOR SUCCESS

MONTH ELEVEN

This is the penultimate month of your year of goal-setting. Make sure this month brings about the most success. What is the one thing you would like to change but have been daunted by the challenge, that one thing is what you are going to tackle this month. Come on, you can do this. Don't take the easy option, take on a challenge!

Write your goal below:

Is it SMART?

Is your goal specific?	Yes/No	Explain how is it specific?	
Is your goal measurable?	Yes/No	How can you measure it?	
Is your goal achievable?	Yes/No	How do you know this?	
Is your goal realistic?	Yes/No	How can you tell?	
Is your goal within a timeframe of this month?	Yes/No	Can you do this in one month?	

If you've amended your goal to make it SMART, write your smarter goal below:

Now sign below to commit to your goal and write today's date and when you are going to review it:

Signed:

Today's date:

To be reviewed: (put one month's time)

REFLECT, REVIEW, GOAL-SET

MONTH ELEVEN

So, how did you do? Let's make a few notes below:

What did you find easy about working towards your goal?

What did you find difficult?

When you found things difficult, how did thinking about your grit factor and mindset help?

What would you do differently next time?

What are you most proud of in the last month?

So, to summarise, last month you set yourself a goal for self-improvement using the grit you have developed. Now, let's see how you did.

My goal in the last month was to:

I achieved my goal because:

I did not achieve my goal because:

What I have learnt about myself, my grit and my mindset in the last month:

My mission next month is to improve my performance and success in the following area:

Well done you for setting yourself a really challenging goal. You know that we make the most progress when we find things hard. If you only do things you find easy, you won't stretch yourself and accelerate your progress. Always embrace a challenge!

GOAL-SETTING FOR SUCCESS

LOOKING TO THE FUTURE – MONTH TWELVE

Just think of all the things you have achieved in the last 12 months – you have come so far because of your grit and determination. This is by no means the end of your journey, this is simply the beginning. It is now time for you to move forward and continue to use goal-setting as a tool for change on your own. What I want you to do this month is set a goal that sets out how and when you are going to goal-set in the future to ensure you make it a regular habit. This is now your time to fly and become the best you can.

Write below a goal which challenges you to reflect, review and goal-set in the future. Make sure it is SMART!

Looking to the future, I will set goals in the following way...

Now sign below to commit to your goal and write today's date and when you are going to review it:

Signed:

Today's date:

To be reviewed:

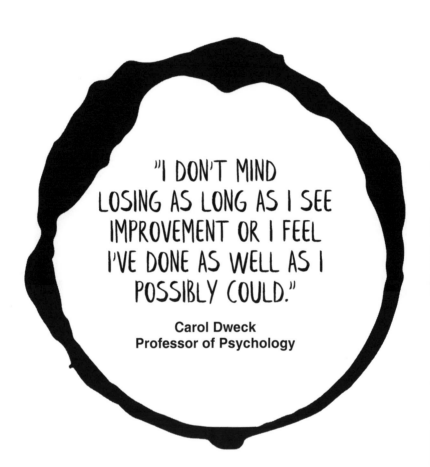

"I DON'T MIND LOSING AS LONG AS I SEE IMPROVEMENT OR I FEEL I'VE DONE AS WELL AS I POSSIBLY COULD."

Carol Dweck
Professor of Psychology

Truly remarkable – yes that is what you are.

You have shown so much commitment, passion and dedication over the last year. You should be so very proud of yourself. You have achieved a great deal using your grit, and by regularly reflecting on your strengths and weaknesses you have brought about success in all areas of your life.

I now hope you continue to demonstrate grit by extending this process of reflection, review and goal-setting to ensure you continue to exceed your potential.

Now time for your final entry into this Grit Journal from you. Drum roll please...

My name is _____ and I am incredibly proud to have used My Grit Journal to achieve the following successes in my academic, personal and social life over the last year:

I think everyone should use My Grit Journal because:

Now take a photo of the above and share it on social media to inspire others to achieve as you have using the hashtag **#MyGritJournal**

Don't forget to tag me so I can see how well you've done.

Facebook **@MrsBrownWriter**
Twitter **@MrsBrownWriter**
Instagram **@MrsBrownWriter**

I would love to hear more from you about how My Grit Journal has helped you achieve your goals and what your aspirations for the future are. Drop me a line at **hello@mrsbrown.me** – it would be great to hear about your goals and successes. You can also check out my website to find out more about grit, growth and success at **www.mrsbrown.me**

You are a star and you have shown that, because of your grit, you are able to set goals, overcome difficulties and achieve success no matter what challenge you are faced with.

Just brilliant, well done! Keep up the good work.

Best wishes,

Kerry

Printed in Germany
by Amazon Distribution
GmbH, Leipzig

18522999R10089